# GUARDIAN ANGEL
## A Collection of Poems

## *By Laura Fitton*

Published by The Solopreneur Publishing Company Ltd., West Yorkshire.

The Solopreneur Publishing Company Ltd focuses on the needs of each individual author client. This book has been published through their 'Solopreneur Self-Publishing (SSP)' brand that enables authors to have complete control over their finished book whilst utilising the expert advice and services usually reserved for traditionally published print, in order to produce an attractive, engaging, quality product. Please note, however, that final editorial decisions and approval rested with the author.

ISBN 978-1-8382502-0-1

Printed in the U.K.

***In memory of my best friend, Sofie.***

*Thank you for your belief in me and guidance. Thank you for a wonderful friendship over the years, your continuous belief in my abilities and support, for making me laugh and smile. This year you would have joined me in the thirties club, so this one is our birthday gift to you!*
*Always in our hearts.*

*With Love, Laura and Billy xxx*

### With Special thanks to ...

My family, My Mum Sue, My Dad Rob and my Sister
Hayley, and of course, the boys - Billy and Jimmy. For their
support with my writing over the years. I have made you all
laugh and cry on numerous occasions. To Adam for saying
get them published and giving me a kick up the backside.

I have to give these guys a shout out. Michael, you came
into my life when Sofie died, you saw me at my worst and
stuck around and then saw me at my best. You won the
title vote! Thanks for your contribution.

Robyn and Kirsty, my two Musketeers, you really do not
know how much you mean to me. Deborah, for keeping me
sane and focused and fully supportive of every decision I
have made.

Rima, for believing in me when I didn't. Loubie Lou and
Sue, for dragging me out of the house, taking me dancing
when I needed to clear my head, and for injecting fun back
into my life.

I want to thank my counsellor, Gita, who also supported
me through one of my dark times. You helped me to see
the light. You always believed that I should get my work
published one day and that I should at least try. I did say

you can have the massive mind map you had me writing for your wall.

To my army of angels, nurses, specialists, and doctors who inspire me every day, to my team. For steering us safely through the COVID Pandemic. Thank you for your continuous support.

For all your support and advice to my publisher, Gail. For guiding a newbie on a special journey with a project that means so much. I love it.

The list of thanks is never-ending, as I am grateful to so many. I want to thank you all for your support over the years. The following book of poems is what we created.

*With Love*
*Laura xx*

# Foreword

Some people say that writers write their best stuff from influential life events. Guardian Angel is a compilation of poems that I have written over the years. They are personal, and they are from the heart.

I touch upon topics that people find difficult to talk about, such as death and dying, the grieving process, and the feeling of huge loss.

My poems come to me. I cannot spontaneously on the spot write them. They may come to me when I am sleeping and when I'm relaxing listening to music. It surprises me what I see in front of me when I put my pen down.

I have merged my two passions. I have touched on my career as a nurse. I have written about Dementia after experiencing a whole shift caring for one lady who had it. I wrote the COVID poem when I was suffering from it.

I give my two Lhasa Apso dogs Billy and Jimmy, a voice, as I do look at them sometimes and wonder what they think and feel. After a cuddle on my knee, one-day, the poem came to me.

At work, I was looking after my gran on the ward where I worked and where she died. It was a challenge going back to work as my gran and I were very close. My personal favourite is *"I'll meet you in the clearing..."* That poem came to me in a dream, and as soon as I woke, I wrote it down.

I have written about being the victim of an abusive domestic relationship. How hard it is to get out of a relationship. The struggles I faced and my family at the time. It can take a while to tell people, but there is help and support all around.

My friends and family play a big part in my writing. I touch on relationships with my grandparents from being little to as we got older. I have written poems for my best friends.

The book itself is dedicated to my best friend, who sadly died before she turned 21. I also tell her story to raise awareness to help stop people drink driving. She bought me a gift of a Guardian Angel statue before she died. I genuinely believe she is my Guardian Angel. My close circle of friends helped me to choose the fitting title.

'Guardian Angel' can make you laugh, it can make you smile, and it can make you cry.

I believe in Angels...I believe we all have someone watching over us... don't you?

My patients, family, and friends have always pushed me to try and get published. I decided to take matters into my own hands.

*Enjoy!*

# Contents

# Through My Dog's Eyes -
# A Poem for My Mummy

*A soft pad of paws, my stomping feet,*
*She's said my favourite words. Do you want a treat?*
*I wish I were human, and I had a voice too,*
*As I'd shout from the rooftops, "Mummy, I Love You!"*

*When I am with my mummy, the fun does not end,*
*How I wish I could tell you that you're my best friend.*
*She thinks she's clever and taught me some Spanish,*
*Little does she know she has not; I only twitch my head to*
*acknowledge.*

*She has said the word Queso. It means cheese, I think...*
*So, I'll just sit still and stare at her if I can, trying not*
*to blink.*
*I follow her all over, and I get under her feet,*
*Waiting for her to sit down as her knees are my seat.*

*I snuggle her to keep her warm, and I plant a kiss on*
*her nose,*
*I can smell her perfume, I sneeze, and "EWWW" she goes.*
*I love Mummy time; I guard her through the night,*
*She also protects me when the fireworks give me a fright.*

1

*I lull her to sleep, the cheek of her! She moans when I snore,*
*I think how rude! I carry on and ignore.*
*My little brother Jimmy, I will tease him to get him to play,*
*Sometimes he wants to if he is feeling mischievous one day.*

*We race around Daddy's garden stepping on his handiwork,*
*Peeing on his soil, pooing on his grass, we drive him berserk.*
*Caravan holidays are simply the best,*
*We can be tired from all the walking; our little legs ache, and*
*we just want to rest.*

*I don't think Mama is embarrassed pushing us in our own*
*pushchair,*
*Only when we get out to walk again, and there's nothing left*
*in there.*
*We stop at the Suncastle Bar, any excuse for a beer,*
*We listen to the sound of the waves crashing in our ear.*

*My Aunty Hayley is trying to set us up on a date,*
*A little doggy that belongs to her mate.*
*We are very well mannered, I've learnt that from Mum,*
*However, the little pooch is offended when Jimmy sniffs her*
*bum.*
*He hasn't got the coolness that I have you see,*
*A cheeky little smile that will make your heart melt for me.*

*I love my life and, of course, my family too,*
*I wouldn't change it for the world, would you?*
*Surrounded by my family, full of love, food, toys,*
*and Ted Ted,*
*Now I bid you goodnight, as I am off to my bed.*

*Goodnight.*
*Lots of love Billy x*

# My Lhasa Apso Nephew Jimmy

Watching, waiting, ready to pounce,
A running rampage through the house.
You wait for the thud of something he'll hit,
Instead, you hear Mum screaming, "Oh My God He's Shit!"
It's under the bed; it's near the top.
Then you hear, "ROB! Come and do your job!"
Jimmy is running towards me; he's running away,
Now he thinks he can just play.
He sniffs, he licks, he smiles at you,
"Jimmy, you are in so much trouble." He's so adorable too.
Little black rubber lips that tickle your palm,
This, is my bright-eyed, mischievous nephew, Jim Jam.

# Being a Nurse is an Honour

Nursing isn't just a job; it's a passion,
Where comfort comes first, not fashion.
Nurses are people who care,
We let strangers know that we are there.
Some shifts can be extremely tough,
Especially when some of our patients get rough.
Sometimes we sit and ask ourselves, why?
After a shift, we can sit at home, we just cry.
But through the good and the bad times, as a team,
we stay strong,
As alongside our patients is where we belong.
A patient's battle is one we will help fight,
All through the day and during the night.
We always strive to give one hundred percent,
Even when our energy is spent.
From admission to discharge, we give the best,
Even to those who we lay to rest.
Losing a patient is difficult, I will tell you,
We are not robots; we are human, and we do feel it too.
Although it is challenging, it is rewarding, and it can be
fun,
Knowing we are doing our best and getting our jobs done.
A thank you is never too far away,
Those two words can make our day.

We come to work with a smile, that doesn't necessarily always stay,
But we are here to look after you 24 hours a day.

# A Mentor's Promise to a Student Nurse

I may work you hard and encourage you to rest,
I'll teach you all I know as I want you to be the best.
I'll provide you with a perfect environment for you to
work in,
With plenty of opportunities to enhance your learning.
I'll prepare you to qualify, as I know it can be scary,
I'll put my faith in you, so you're as ready as you'll ever be.
My door will be open to offer you honest advice,
To guide you in making the right choice.
You may feel you have no direction and no clue where
to go,
Just follow your heart, and in time, you will know.
Set your goals and challenge yourself; it may well
surprise you,
No matter where you are in the future, I'll be here to
support you.
As a mentor signing you off to qualify is so rewarding,
Even more so when you get a mention, and I hear you're
succeeding.
I love being a mentor; you work me hard, keeping me on
my toes,
Through my teaching, I do hope this shows.
I'll always remember my first day qualifying,
I completely understand how you are feeling.

My mentors gave me sound advice that I care to share,
"Believe in yourself and your abilities, one day, you will find an area that
you love, and you will shine there."
Good Luck

# I Am Just a Lady with Dementia, That's All

*My name is Laura, I am an eighty-year-old female,*
*Now spare me some time and hear my tale.*
*I am a wrinkled shell so frail and old,*
*Beneath the confusion lies a heart of gold.*

*I have Dementia, a terrible disease,*
*Which makes people around me feel ill at ease.*

*My memories are stored in chronological order,*
*Merged into such a muddle, no separation by border.*
*My youthful memories are as clear as day,*
*It is my recent ones that have faded away.*

*I remember going to school way back then,*
*Playing with my best friend, Ben.*
*I remember my very first kiss,*
*Surrounded by important people, who I now dismiss.*

*But ask me what happened an hour ago, of course,*
*I will struggle,*
*Because all my memories are in one hell of a muddle.*
*Sometimes I do panic, and I do shout for my mum,*
*And some people tell me that she will come.*

*Well...hmm... I'm eighty-odd,*
*She isn't going to come, you silly sod.*
*My mother is dead,*
*That memory is lost, gone right out of my head.*

*My feelings of loss and upset, they still haunt me now,*
*But attaching that emotion to the right memory, I can't*
*somehow.*

*One thing to remember is, please do not lie to me,*
*I remember everything you will soon see.*
*Please tell me the truth, even if it hurts me, you must,*
*One day it may piece itself together again, and I remember,*
*it's you I'll not trust.*

*When I have been unwell in hospital they'll whisper behind*
*my back,*
*Just give me a few minutes, will you, to get my thoughts*
*back on track.*
*When I am scared, yes...I do shout out,*
*But how on earth would you feel with complete strangers*
*about?*

*I cannot remember how I got here; I want to go home,*
*All these people around me, yet I feel so alone.*

*I love walking around; I am very steady, I promise I*
*won't fall,*
*I am not a prisoner in this institution, no, not at all!*
*I am instantly told to sit back in my chair,*
*There is only so long you can sit down and stare.*

*People look at me like I am a freak out of space,*
*Ha! And you wonder why I want to escape from this place?*

*Uncomfortable, lonely and I am scared too,*
*Please let me go home, this I do beg you.*
*Back to my bungalow where everything is neat,*
*Ah! My recliner chair and a pouffe for my feet.*
*Surrounded by my photographs and belongings of my own,*
*Now I do not feel so alone.*

*So next time I am poorly or unwell, and I require a little help*
*from you,*
*Here's another thing to bear in mind too.*
*I am not just a wrinkled old shell with a terrible disease,*
*I am a lady with feelings who could put you at ease.*

## A Cancer Scare

I don't even know what to think,
I don't even know what to feel,
What I do know is that my heart will sink,
If what this could be turns out to be real.

Fear is just an emotion that I should easily brush away,
Playing games with the thoughts in my mind,
I'm anxiously sitting patiently waiting for Monday,
Although the answer I seek I will not find.

I'm surrounded by good people who I clearly love,
Some I may not have known that long,
I have my Guardian Angels up above,
All working together, they're keeping me strong.

Keep positive; I'll try my best,
It doesn't help knowing what it could be,
Hopefully, soon they will test,
And a positive outcome I will see.

Thank you for being there,
And being here for me every step of the way,
It is a good feeling knowing that you care,
If ever there comes a time when you need me, I will be there
that day.

# When Death is Close

When you're with someone nearing the end,
They've no family around; you're becoming their friend.
A glimpse in their eyes, you can see all their fears,
A heart-breaking sight that can move you to tears.
When they hold your hand, not wanting to let go,
It comes to a point where you realise that they know.
Their colour changes and fades away,
They may have many thoughts but unable to find words
to say.
They grip your hand tight,
You reassure them that everything will be alright.
Offer them whispers of love and encouragement and to try
to relax,
You give them a hug, and around you, their arm wraps.
You feel their tension ease, and their body unwind,
As the stress and fear of dying leaving their mind.
You go back to holding hands until they peacefully rest
and sleep,
A peaceful smile crosses their face; slowly it'll creep.
Your duty is fulfilled, you leave the room, as they're
peaceful,
Revert to a corner, compose yourself as your eyes are
tearful.

# Covid-19- A Silent Killer

A virus from China named Covid-19,
That's terrorised the world, an invisible enemy,
remaining unseen.
Medics sent to War wearing a mask and an overall,
We have witnessed the young and the fittest of folk fall.

You attack their respiratory system and move on through
their body,
They're not allowed visitors, loved ones, nobody.
You've isolated them, and they must fight you alone,
Some will kick you out of their system until you have gone.

Some of the victims are very frail and old,
Some of them fall as you take a strong hold.
Was your intention to cause such heartbreak and to kill?
Or, simply to make some of us ill?

The upset and devastation you caused worldwide will never
be gone,
You have even robbed us of our freedom.
You have crept silently into our lives, filling us with fear,
We cannot even hug our loved ones as then we are too
near.

Two metres apart, we are told we must stay,

The mental stress and mind games you continue to play.
Unfortunately, many thousands of lives you have taken, we
could not save,
The strength and courage they bravely tried to fight you,
their all, they gave.


I, myself I have fought you, with an underlying respiratory
disease,
I prayed every night for it to remain dormant, Please...
You drained my energy and made me so lethargic,
You floored me; I was so sick.


I avoided hospital admission; I fought you at home,
Unable to breathe is frightening when you're alone.
I am a frontline warrior, a nurse, and we never give in,
Your days are numbered Covid-19, were coming.


Scientists and medics looking for cures and treatments,
searching worldwide,
Are you scared yet, silent killer? With nowhere to hide.
You are going to be eliminated; you have made history
that's for sure,
Vaccines, medicinal trials, we are closing in on a cure.

The day you are eliminated, we all unite and sit patiently, and we wait,
To hold our loved ones and to celebrate.
We'll hold a minute's silence for those who paid the ultimate cost,
Remembering and honouring our loved ones, who sadly we have lost.

Enough now! Covid-19! Our battle will be won!
A cure is coming to get you, so if I were you, I'd run!

# Have You Ever Felt Loneliness Burning?

Have you ever felt loneliness burning?
Surrounded by nothing, it's love that your yearning.
You do everything to please people and try your best,
But they are quick to drop you, just like the rest.
You can sacrifice, and you can give your all, even your life,
To someone who used to make you happy, your future wife.
I can be quiet, lost and in painful memories from my past,
I wish a bomb would go off in my head sometimes, off
they'd blast.
I am constantly hurting, but I have no idea why,
I give things a go; I do try.
It is never enough I'm still left alone with nothing around,
People will wonder why I am so sunken into the ground.

# A Domestic Abuse Victim - Survivor Story

Now I am free,
From the pain, abuse, and torture that you showed me.
It went so deep that I had lost my ability to write my poems
to cope,
It was like you tightened the noose and pulled the rope.

People ask me why I stayed,
It was extremely difficult to break free from the mental
mind games you both played.
At the beginning, I genuinely believed that this was real,
You convinced me of a future, that my dreams would come
true, and it was love that I'd feel.

I remember the threats to my family, not long after my gran
died,
Your Ex did that, and my parents and family cried.
People question then Laura, why didn't you walk?
As the grief gave me some confidence, I could answer back;
I could talk.

During those times, you never actually defended me,
Late-night abusive phone calls around two or three.
You said that I accepted that your Ex was your friend,
That I did, but if my friend behaved in this way, that
friendship would sure end.

When you were back in London, you'd meet her and get
drunk on a night out,
Even then, the next day you'd beg my forgiveness, and the
broken promises came out.
Blame it on the alcohol and unawareness, but you really
could not care,
But my sixth sense told me you were being unfaithful and
unfair.

When I said I was gone, I wanted to break up; I wanted to
leave,
Another web of abuse and false apologies you would weave.
You'd suck me back in; I would get a few days of niceness,
Then, after that, you reverted to making me feel worthless.

My parents and family saw you begin to socially isolate me,
They tried their goddam hardest to make me see.
You manipulated me against all my friends and family
members nearby,
Making me doubt sound relationships, where I felt alone to
the point I would cry.

You wanted me as yours, and yours only, everything I had
you took,
You went to the extremes of threatening my mate Michael
and blocking him on Facebook.

I thought he was being the nice lad that he is and stepped
back, where we lost touch,
It was a couple of years later I realised what you had done,
and I had missed so much.


My pen pal, I had a great friendship with a girl in Spain,
Who supported me more than you did when my grief
returned again?
She called me on WhatsApp in London. Can you remember
that?
She put you in your place, and you ensured that friendship
went flat.


She had her own cancer battle to fight, and we spoke of
normal stuff instead,
She isn't here now; you cut off her support network, you
are sick in the head.
She knew I wanted to get out, and she tried her best to help
me,
She said I had to stay safe, a moment will come, and I had
to wait patiently.


My parents said,
If I do not get out of that relationship, I will end up dead.
I didn't dare tell them that was the only way out that I saw
in my head!

I was outnumbered even your mates joined in,
If I were behaving the way you were, my mates would have
given me a good kickin'.
When your Ex beat me up in Southall, you left me all alone,
To me, that was my ticket out of this; it was done.

It left me having severe flashbacks, where I would just
freeze,
When I came home to Doncaster, I panicked when I had to
leave the house. I couldn't breathe.
I still have them now, and I do not know when they will go,
But you don't condone that event if you loved me no.

If I pressed charges, you threatened my job to which I'd
lose,
You said you'd make such a story; they would believe you,
and I wouldn't have the option to choose.
It still was not the right time to leave, as I didn't feel safe
yet,
I locked it in my mind, not even attempting to forget.

People thought we were okay in Wales when we went on
holiday,
I didn't realise by capturing a rail in a photograph would
send more abuse my way.
"You're useless; you can't even take a fucking photograph

right!"
You were in my face, angry. I thought you were going to hit
me; you gave me a fright.

Driving home from Snowdonia, complete silence, tears on
my face, thoughts racing in my head,
You rang your mate Pamela, spoke in creole, so I didn't
have a clue what was said.
Not long after this, I tried to break free,
You harassed me and wouldn't leave me alone; I couldn't
believe.

You were driving me berserk,
You even tried getting me at one place I felt safe, by calling
me at work.
I ended up going back to you, as I was not strong enough to
stay out,
That's when my counselling came about.

It was mainly for the flashbacks, but as my story started to
spill,
She showed me stuff on domestic abuse and told me to
read it if I will.
My eyes filled with tears, as I saw myself there, and I'd cry,
She was so relieved that I reacted like that, and she told me
why.

You're a victim of abuse, and if you don't get out, you could
be in danger,
She showed me clues of behaviour changes, and it was a
complete game-changer.

She told me that the old me was still there, hidden inside,
Like a wounded animal trying to recover so, they'll curl up
and hide.
After eight months of counselling I got my confidence, my
strength back, and I saw the light,
Which gave me the strength to finally end it one night.

The aftermath, she helped me more, as my head and my
heart were colliding,
The mind games and emotional blackmail that followed
were magnifying.
It would have been a quieter life for me to go back,
I had come this far forward; my life was on the right track.

Deep down, I still believed she loved me, and I didn't know
why?
When it was all just one big lie.
I am finally free! That I can clearly shout,
Thank god, I did it before lockdown, as I would never have
been able to get out.

You'd have me suffer and totally mess up my head,
My parents' worry may have come true, and the result
would be me being dead.
I feel sorry for those in my position who haven't managed to
get out,
There is help about!

I really hope you have learnt a lesson, and your next victim
won't be treated this way,
You didn't take everything I've worked hard for; you'll see
this one day.
It would be quite funny if ever I were to see you at Gay
Pride,
You tried to break my friendships, you went to great
lengths, but they'd be there by my side.

You should never have underestimated me and my friends
and my love for my family,
As the 'real', Laura would defend them until I die, and now
I can live my life happily.
I personally want to thank each of them for standing by me.
It must have been hell; you endured it too,
From the bottom of my heart, you saved me, and all my
love goes out to every one of you.

## A Flashback to Southall - my memory returned.

The night before your birthday, I had an idea, and it felt so right,
I'd get up bright and early and hit the road before daylight.
I was up showered and dressed nicely, cake and gifts in the car by 2 a.m.
I started my three and a half-hour drive down the A1/M.

The road was quiet. I was so excited I felt sick,
I wasn't expected till this afternoon. I was happy and singing to my music.
As I drove closer, I was giddy, and I wondered what else could I do?
I was starving, so I stopped at McDonald's, and I bought breakfast for me and you.

I drove to your workplace in Southall, I came and knocked at the door,
It may have been shock or fear on your face because your jaw hit the floor.
I passed you your breakfast, and you reminded me you were fasting,
Ah, yes, sorry I kept forgetting.

I wished you a happy birthday,
You gave me a hug and a kiss and said thank you for
coming all this way.
I said, "I'll drop you home, and you can still do what you
planned to do.
As whilst you do that, there's stuff I can be doing too."

I walked back to my car where I'd eat, sit and wait,
I saw Rima was online, so I'd video call my mate.
I checked in, we caught up, as at this time she was off sick,
Little did we know what a moment we would pick...

BANG! BANG! BANG! BANG! A fist hammering my car
window,
I screamed so loud, and she said, "What are you doing here
bitch? Sod off and go!"
Rima asked, "who on earth is she?"
I said she's my partner's ex-girlfriend, the one that's been
causing issues for my family and me.

She stormed from my car and headed to the door, pure
anger on her face,
Once my heart rate had calmed down, I left my car to stand
my ground, as now was the place.
Rima, on the line, I felt safe; I walked to the door, "What's
going on?"

My partner replied, "Laura, you must leave right now. Be gone!"

The door slammed in my face with the two of them behind it,
I panicked as I couldn't protect her, oh shit.
She always said if she saw me, she'd kill me. I joked to Rima, "maybe now is the time?"
She's jealous my family accepted my sexuality, hers no, but mine are fine.

I said to Rima, "she's probably beating her up. I'm not leaving. I'm gonna wait."
"Did you see the size of her, Laura be careful, won't you mate."
I waited half an hour, and they reappeared; it was a moment of madness,
I saw the gash on my partner's face. I felt worthless, crushed by a wave of sadness.

"What the hell has she done to you? Look at your face?"
Her ex smirked back at me angrily. I said, "you're a disgrace!"
"This is how you treat someone you love and care for. Is it a few punches you serve?"
I looked my partner in the eye, "whatever is going on, a beating you don't deserve."

Her ex replied, "I saw you. I hate you. And this is what you made me do."

I replied, "you're not my favourite person, love, but you don't see me behaving this way, do you?"

I turned away from her ex and faced my partner now that was my mistake,

As the events that followed caused my whole body to shake.

Scratched my arms and face, grabbed me by the hair and arms, threw me to the floor,

And what followed next will stay with me forever more...

# A Flashback to Southall

*Thrown to the ground, fighting for breath.*
*Head above the pavement staring at death.*
*Solid punches you're smashing into my head.*
*A sickening rhythm which now you've embedded.*
*Don't sleep Laura. Don't sleep, you must stay awake.*
*I wanted to scream, but no noise could I make.*
*Propped up on my elbows. Hands covering my face. What's this about?*
*How many more punches before I blackout?*
*She's not stopping...I am gonna die...oh shit!*
*Thud...Thud...Thud...is this going to be it?*
*Hand on the back of my head. Trying to smash it against concrete.*
*Holding my head up. Can't focus. Trying to defend myself. Come on feet!*
*I replay the alphabet from A to Zed.*
*I am paralysed with fear. How am I not dead?*
*A peek through my fingers. It's blurry. My head is spinning.*
*I am sure that is a woman at the window watching.*
*I am sending silent pleas of help to a stranger.*
*COME ON! MY LIFE IS IN FUCKING DANGER!*
*She is not stopping! Can you not see?*
*I would run and jump to help you if you were me.*
*Who is that screaming? Who is there?*
*Someone answering my prayer.*

*Thud...Thud...Thud...Thud...I feel sick...PANIC!*
*She is not stopping! Whatever you do, please don't kick!*
*Slowing my breathing down. One...Two...Three...*
*You're going to be okay; Laura trust me.*
*Whose voice is that? Gran is that you?*
*Nah! I am gone for sure because that can't be true.*

The punches slowed and eventually stopped, am I alive?
I thought one punch could kill; how did I survive?
I laid still on the floor, head spinning, eyes wide open
unmoving,
I could hear footsteps in the distance away she was
walking.

I sat myself up slowly, where are my sunglasses? They were
on my head,
Snapped into two pieces my favourite, I guess I'll buy new
ones instead.
My partner came to me, crouched in my face, and said,
"you should never have come!"
I felt sure she was going to hold me, but away she would
run.

I looked around me; I was alone. There was no one around.
I stood myself up; I lost my balance and fell back to the
ground.
I managed to get to the car, but I cannot remember how,
I rang Rima back and updated her, and I asked her, "what
now?"

"Ring the police get her reported and let me know how it
goes!
"Where's your partner?" I replied, "who knows?"
I dialled 999, and I locked the doors, and I waited in the
car,
Split lip, scratched face, arms, and bruises, hair all over me
she can't have gone far.

Got no painkillers my head is killing me,
What do I tell the police? I don't know her ex, my only
witness is my partner, and she's gone and left me?
What was she doing in Southall she doesn't live near?
Maybe this is why I was meant to come in the afternoon as
she knew she'd be here.

SURPRISE! HAPPY BIRTHDAY I HOPE YOU HAD A GOOD
ONE!
It completely backfired on me. I cannot believe you've run.
The police came, took photos of my injuries, and concluded

jealousy attack,
They rang my partner to tell her to come back.


Any witnesses? I explained the lady at the window,
They knocked at the door; it was her...she shook her head
...no.
In the back of the police car giving my statement, my phone
flashed a text,
"Do not press charges. She'll have your job next."


Is she still with her then? I don't have a clue,
Police asked, "Is there anyone I can call to be with you?"
I've driven from Yorkshire; It was a birthday surprise, you
see,
It well and truly backfired on me.


"We're going to investigate this. Do you want to press
charges?"
A jolt of fear shot through me, my job, can I think about
this?
My head was banging and spinning; they completely
understood,
They told me to go to hospital due to the head injury I knew
I should.


"We can dial for an ambulance; it's not that far."

Keep it free for someone who needs it; I'll take the car.
I looked through the window, my partner, a stranger, she
came,
She was speaking to an officer; she gave her own name.

We sat in the car complete silence, her eyes on my face,
"Where's the nearest hospital I need to get out of this
place?"
I started to drive; her phone rang. I cannot believe it's her,
what now?
"Tell her if she presses charges, I'll have her job, can she
hear, it'll happen somehow!"

I didn't react. I drove in silence, thinking just carry on,
I couldn't feel anything, just numbness or show any
emotion.
I parked up, and I walked to A+E; my legs wouldn't support
me, they were wobbly,
She held me up to support me.

I felt sick, "go take a seat, and I'll check you in."
Why all of a sudden are you being so caring?
I wished she'd knocked me unconscious; they'd have rung
my next of kin, my dad,
Imagine receiving that phone call; the drive down could
have ended bad.

She told me, "I told them you went dizzy, you had a fall,
And you've badly hit your head on a wall."
Once again, I was in pure shock,
You're defending her; how hard was your knock?

Three hours wait I wanted to be anywhere but here,
Back in Yorkshire with my family and friends near.
My head in my hands, rocking in pain, tears on my cheek,
I cannot process anything can't even speak.

I was being reviewed a torch shone in my eyes,
My partner did all the speaking LIES! LIES! LIES!
The only thing I can remember is the doctor said no alcohol
to drink,
I thought many a pint I could so easily sink.

Come back for a CT head if you start to spew,
To ensure there is no bleed on the brain, I replied, thank
you.
He gave me some painkillers, which I did take,
Wishing I'd never driven down this morning, what a
mistake.

Which hotel do I stay in? I'm in such a state?
I look at my partner; my feelings of love have turned to
hate.
I dropped her at home, and a hotel I would find,

Panic crept over me; I don't feel safe, flashbacks in my
mind.

Anyone in the next room they'd have heard me crying,
I couldn't get over the fact of her defending and lying.
She met me later on,
After I'd watched the England women's game, I think we
won,

We got a takeaway,
We ate it back at the hotel as inside, I needed to stay.
When I was alone, I had forwarded my wound photos on to
Rima,
I awoke in the night she was looking at the photos on my
phone. I couldn't believe her.

I already had a feeling that she'd try to delete,
that's why I sent them to Rima before; I was thinking on my
feet.
The next day I drove to Dover out of London to clear my
head,
A walk along the white cliffs, fresh air, grateful I'm not
dead.

We still received threats even on that day,
Don't worry, London, I'll be keeping well away.
The photos we took in Dover I kept my bruises well hidden,
As no one was allowed to know what had happened, I was
forbidden.

I couldn't tell my family as my sister was midst of a cancer
scare,
Even though deep down, I knew they'd be there.
I came home to Doncaster carrying the threat of my job,
Little did they realise my freedom they'd rob.

I was scared to leave the house, pure fear inside,
Work was no longer a safe haven; I had nowhere to hide.
I broke down in tears when they commented on my arm,
My emotions flooded me, and I couldn't stay calm.

I told them I'd been jumped the truth I wanted so badly to
spill,
The fear of my job, the threats, what next? In my heart, this
would fill.
The flashbacks to Southall still haunt me to this day,
But now my story is out there, I am hoping to keep them
away.

I got asked, looking back, would I have acted differently or the same?
I'd have acted the same; I'd have tried harder to protect her, so no harm ever came.
I felt proud of myself standing up to a bully,
Even now, I've accepted I'll never understand fully.

I have unanswered questions, the truth, of course, I'd like to know,
I am happy that I walked away and moved on, and eventually the trauma will go.

## Mammar

I had a Grandma who was incredibly special to me,
We went to visit every Sunday and even stayed for tea.
We used to play a family game, and we charged 10p a go,
But when I was waiting for one last number, she went and
shouted BINGO!

I remember singing her a song,
And appearing from behind a curtain.
She used to cheer and clap along,
She used to enjoy it. I knew this for certain.

I remember one Sunday I was sat on her knee,
Talking about when I grow up and about life.
She turned and smiled, she said to me,
You'll make a great housewife.

She said when you grow up, you'll be big and strong,
You're going to be a model and very tall.
This must have been the only time I've known her to be
wrong,
I'm neither of those things, I'm a nurse, and I'm small.

You'll have to forgive me,
This year I am not going to a bonfire tonight,
We have a little dog called Billy,
The fireworks give him an awful fright.

It' been 12 years since you died,
That day is still clear,
I remember it like yesterday, and I cried,
All I wanted to do was hold you near.

When you were here, you taught me many things, most
importantly one,
Be there for other people and let them know you care,
Don't judge or be disrespectful and that I should love
everyone,
I wish everyone could be like that; sometimes, life is not
fair.

All of your qualities and characteristics I hold strong and
true,
They are stored deep within my heart,
They are all of the things that made you, you,
When I do something good, I see you, and we're not really
apart.

When you are watching from your fluffy cloud,
I hope you like what you see,
I hope I am making you proud,
And that you love the person I have turned out to be.

I am the granddaughter of the brightest star,
I have an Angel for a friend,
I know we aren't close, in fact we're far,
I want you to know that my love for you will never end.

# A Birthday Letter to Mammar

To/ Mammar,

Like a ray of sunshine on a rainy day,
Your smile and laughter touched our hearts,
Then you passed on through a cloud and went away,
But were never far apart.

I hold good memories strong and true,
Which make you feel so near,
They pick me up when I'm feeling blue,
I really wish you were here.

Happy Birthday
Miss you lots
Love you with all my heart
Laura.

# A Poem for an Amazing Lady - My Gran

As a child, a weekend stay at Gran and Grandad's was
always a blast,
And those are fond memories stored in my past.
They taught me how to play cards and how to play Rummy,
We never played for real money.


Hayley and I would dance in their kitchen and practice
our show,
Later in the evening, they'd come to watch clapping as
we'd go.
Our meals when we stayed,
Hayley would dread, and she prayed.
Potatoes, swede, carrots all mashed into one, piled high on
her plate,
She wasn't allowed to leave the table until every last bit
she ate.
I was cheeky; I told Gran I was going to keep her company,
Every time I popped in, I'd eat a spoonful, and we'd find it
so funny.
Gran only found out about that last year,
But it made her laugh and shed a tear.
Meat and potato pie, my absolute favourite,
Another meal Hayley hated.

Hayley doesn't like potatoes, but for dessert, it was lemon
pie,
It was bloody delicious, no word of a lie.

We would sit and look at upcoming birthdays to see whose
card we had to buy,
She'd have me writing them in April even if their birthdays
weren't until July.
Don't get me started on Christmas cards, Oh what a chore,
I wrote over a hundred last Christmas. I was thinking how
many more.

Growing up, she'd say, "Laura, you're getting bigger and
bigger,"
I'd say, "I know your shrinking and getting smaller and
shorter."
She'd put her arms around me, for a hug and be up on her
toes,
Even then, she'd only reach my nose.

Even when the pneumonia made her delirious,
She was organising her chaos.
Long list of jobs ironing, washing and don't forget the pots,
If she were lucid, there would have been lots.
She liked to be organised and have everything just so,
You knew where to find everything whenever you'd go.

Gran had the warmest of hearts and purest soul, stumbled
upon Grandad many moons ago,
It was at the fairground where he paid for her a second go.
Growing up with them both has shown me there is
someone for everybody,
With Grandad she found her somebody.


Watching those two bicker and disagree was way better
than watching TV,
It was so funny.
Neither would back down until Grandad gave in,
The cheeky faces she would pull when she'd win.
The love was still present using his nickname 'Nip',
It was in the hospital when she told him to get off her fish
and chip.
You weren't there, Grandad, and neither was the food,
I can assure you she was happy, although pleasantly
confused.


When I saw her at work, everyone's name she would
mention,
Followed by verbal nonsense, even I couldn't work out her
intention.
I was gobsmacked on Saturday; she recognised me, the first
time in over a week,
"Oh! It's Laura." I could not speak.

Her smile was big, and mine was too,
It meant so much, the five minutes of recognition from you.

So, thank you, Gran, for the great times over the years,
Everybody will have their own memories that'll help them
dry up their tears.

## Lost Without You Gran

Everyone is planning Christmas; I can't this year!
As I have lost one special lady, I held so dear.
I even knew what I was buying you for Christmas; you'd
have loved it,
A Strictly Come Dancing ticket.
We'd have gone for dinner, of course, to the pub,
And watch the show we both know we'd love.

But I need to stop running and accept that you have gone,
Accept that people around me feel the same. I'm not the
only one.
I thought I was doing okay; I kept busy and distracted,
But what a spontaneous prat I have acted.
The manic workouts were the best,
Didn't help at all with the grief and the stress.
It gave me the body of a God for our holiday,
I hope you saw; I cracked my fear of flying I was a nervous
wreck the whole way.

Then, I bought a house and moved out,
Mum and Dad, "Are you sure you're ready?" They'd shout.
Grandad tried, "You'll be lonely,"
I was like *I love my own company.*

I've put your photo in my conservatory, yes, its painted
bright pink,
I remember you saying, "to make the boys wink."
It always made me smile somehow,
Especially when I came out, you said, "I can't say that to
you now."

As time passes, it's much harder; it's not easy,
Got nothing now to keep me busy.
I've hit a standstill with nothing to do,
So, I stay wrapped up in our memories, just me and you.
Some I can smile and giggle out loud,
Some I have created since, and I wonder if you're proud.

Then I get the crushing heartbreak because I want you
back,
Your wise words and advice that'd keep me on track.
A chat and a gossip over a cup of tea,
The warmth of your hugs full of love that you gave me.
Taking you off and mocking you,
Making you giggle too.
The list of jobs I'd have waiting when I visit,
I used to drive wondering what is it?

I am out of a job this year Gran, none of your Christmas
cards to write,
Think we managed over a hundred last year, am I right?
My hand was aching at the end,
But every single one we'd send.
Even you didn't know the names, just number 44,
I said, "are there spies living behind that door?"

I am angry, I am tired, sad, and hurt too,
All because I am missing you.
I go to the flat it feels empty and bare,
It's just not the same, not seeing you there.
It's hard for me, I dread to think how Grandad must feel,
Because to me, this is still not real.

I can't cry I feel I have to be strong, as I know I'll not stop
at all,
I have no idea how to bounce back from this heavy fall.
I know this is grief, and I have to give in,
I am not ready to accept that it is you that I am losing.

# Silent Emotions – Returning to Work

I want to stop flashing back to that day,
Where you drifted peacefully asleep and went away.
It's so vivid I can see sights, hear sounds, smell scents, feel the tears,
Hear the voices of everyone stood around you so near.

I was sat in the office when Grandad had his time,
Hayley stood at the door, said, "You'd gone." I said no, you're fine.

I went to the room, and you were so peacefully asleep,
My goodness, how many tears we would weep.
Then I flashback to the room where we all sat,
Lost in our thoughts, trying to process that.
And then it flashes back to the beginning of this poem, replaying, I'm trapped.

Gran, I spiralled, and struggling, I bet you're wanting to give me a good shake,
Cursing me at what a mess I can make.
I've been avoiding everyone around me and pushing them away,
It's not my best move, I see that, but I can't ask them to stay.

I've spoken to a counsellor, yes me, can you believe?
A different perspective she has made me see.


With you in the room and what she said was so true,
I was safe with you near, no fear, and I'm not ready to let go
of you.
That is why they are so vivid because that room is where we
stay,
My heart won't let go or allow me to walk away.


She said, the next session she's breaking that loop and
trying to get it to stop,
I'm so bloody scared I wish she would not.
Is she going to put me under hypnosis, make me walk out
of the room for real?
I am so not ready for that pain that I am going to feel.
One day I'll be ready to walk out and to close that door,
Now, the pain is too real, and I cannot take anymore.


I am getting angry, no explanation, I don't know why you
know I don't have a temper to lose,
I signed up to the gym; I hit a punch bag, and boy, did it
bruise.
I made a mess of my hand and my God, it was bloody sore,
I couldn't stand the pain and frustration anymore.

I don't regret having you near me at work, not at all,
My colleagues loved you; they had a ball.
I hated seeing you confused and talking in your sleep,
On a night shift, I'd come stand by your bedside so quietly
I'd creep.
I'd whisper I love you, walk away and return back to my
role,
The silent pain I would feel, I never told a soul.

That moment of recognition you gave me was the best of
the two weeks,
I was stunned into silence; I could not even speak.
Your eyes lit up; you gave me a big hug filled with love,
It sent my heart soaring with joy way up high above.
I am comforted by that thought, so thank you so much,
It is my personal golden moment that no one can touch.

I still love my job and my team,
At work, I cannot act anymore. My emotions have been
seen.
Sometimes I can go day by day like any other,
It doesn't cause me any bother.
Sometimes I can walk onto the ward, and the flashbacks
will begin,
My emotions start stirring, and I am crying within.
I withdraw, I stay silent, and towards staff, I'm abrupt too,

I can cry fresh tears, as in my mind, its real and happening again to you.

I have supportive colleagues; it's not a weakness to accept their help too,
As they share the funny stories, I didn't hear that actually came from you.

I'm sorry I've been grumpy and grouchy, showing them this I hope they will understand,
I am even ready to accept that helping hand.
I know I am going to be okay and that I will get through it,
I acknowledge the worst is yet to come. I am just awaiting that hit.

I am waiting for Laura to come back, whole and in one piece, to be me,
Then I will be strong enough to focus on our good memories.

## "I'll Meet You in the Clearing..."

*In my dream, we were sat on a bench,*
*And oh my, how my heart did clench.*
*I was sound asleep with a tear running down my face,*
*A conversation with you, I don't want to erase.*

*I was running through a forest shouting, "GRAN!"*
*Over branches, in between trees, so fast I ran.*
*There in a clearing on a bench, you were sat,*
*I came and sat beside you, and we started to chat.*

*Holding my hand, our conversation did flow,*
*I explained to you that I didn't want to let go.*
*You smiled and laughed at me, and you said that I need to,*
*But don't be afraid to do so, as I am right here beside you.*

*I even told you what I was buying you for Christmas,*
*Strictly Come Dancing tickets, you said, "Dam, I missed it."*
*You said I should still go,*
*"Go on, take your Mum and go enjoy the show."*

*You told me to keep smiling and to stay strong,*
*That you will come and visit me soon, it won't be that long.*
*I asked you what you thought of my new house,*
*You said, "Oooo...it's as quiet as a mouse."*

*You stood up; you gave me a big tight hug and a kiss, then you'd disappear,*
*Slowly but surely in crept the fear.*
*A breeze caused a rustle. I sat and watched the sway of a tree,*
*A whisper in my ear, "I am always with you, you'll see."*

# Grandad

I made you a promise which I keep,
That when your time comes, you'll be comfortable and
sleep.
You'll have peace of mind, and you won't be scared,
Surrounded by those who once you cared.
It's painful to watch you slipping away,
It's selfish of us to think, give us one more day.
You're still smiling and grinning; you seem happy right
now,
We'd love to see what you're seeing, but we don't know how.
It's a funny one Grandad, as we don't have a clue,
Whatever is playing, though, is a comfort to you.


Memories come flooding back that are pure gold,
When I remember you and Gran younger, then growing old.
Our walks over the years up Denaby Crags,
Then walking back from the market carrying our bags.
Our trips to Morrisons, on Sunday, before our tea,
You, Gran, Hayley, and Me.
Listening to old songs in the car, laughing at the next track,
Gran, Hayley, and I laughing at your singing behind your
back.
I remember Shirelles, *Will You Still Love Me Tomorrow*
blasting,

You asked me how I knew it? I said off Dirty Dancing.
I sang along with you. What a duet!
Gran and Hayley were laughing that much their tears,
making their cheeks wet.

Playing Rummy in the lounge I am certain you made your
own rules,
As whenever I play that elsewhere, I'm guaranteed to lose.
Every mealtime, you'd say, "I like an empty plate,"
Did you not realise how long it took Hayley to clear it? It
was a long wait.
I used to go help her eat it a little bit,
Otherwise, she would still be sat there now like a right
hermit.

We all sat down in the lounge, heads in a book,
A peep over mine at you both and Gran would send me a
cheeky look.
These were the golden memories that make me genuinely
happy,
And moments that would unite us as a family.
Thank you for the laughs, banter, and good times you gave
me,
In return, I'll ensure you are peaceful and comfortable, that
I promise, you will be.

## My Best Friend Sofie - Our Story

I try not to miss you as I wake up every day,
But as time passes, there are more things I want to say.
It kills me daily that you aren't here with me,
And you cannot have the future you dreamt of and all the
things you wanted to achieve.

It doesn't get any easier, nine years on. It is still very raw,
I no longer believe you can move on from losing your best
friend anymore.
I'd give everything for a few more years with you,
Just to watch you achieve all the things you wanted to.

To watch you walk down the aisle and I'd make the most
embarrassing speech ever,
Where you'd kick me under the table, threaten you'd not
speak to me forever.
To see you have children, as what a great mum you would
be,
Booking my babysitting duties and playing cool aunty.

Having lots of ups and downs through life, no doubt along
the way,
But our friendship was enough to survive them all and
smile every day.

The laughs, the giggles, the moans, and the rants too,
Challenges, crazy ideas, overactive imaginations, I think the
future would have been colourful, don't you?

Ha! Do you remember when I told you I was gay?
You were in pure shock! And replied, "I don't even know
what to say?"
I was the first person you met who was, and you looked at
me like something from space,
It cracks me up, remembering the expression on your face.
In all honestly, you were cool. You wanted me to settle
down with a nice girl and spill the beans to you about,
I told you, "Whoa! Hold ya horses girly; I've not even
properly come out!"

What would we be doing now if you were still around?
Listening to trance music with surround sound?
You said you'd show me how to move to trance music as I
was stiff as a board,
If I'd have tried to move to those beats girly, quite surely I'd
have been floored.

I wonder if I'd have been fluent in Dutch by now as you
taught me a little bit,
In all honesty, my Spanish is ace. My French is crap, so my
Dutch would possibly be shit.

I still remember the plans you made for your 21st birthday,
a bike ride around Oostende as you were determined to
prove I was unfit,
Followed by a trip to the lighthouse, a meal with your
family, and then the clubs we would hit.
It is hard to accept that we couldn't do just that because
my what a 21st to remember,
Unfortunately, you were not here on that day in 2011 on
the 6th of November.

To think on this day, you were riding to college on your bike
like any other,
And that drunk driver hit you and run you over.
I still try and raise awareness "Think Before You Drink,"
As actions can change people's lives like ours in a blink.

They don't see the devastation that they have left behind,
The months of waiting for you to awake from your coma,
friends, and family losing their mind.
They don't see that we have everything crossed waiting for
you to awake,
And we keep fooling ourselves that it was a nightmare or to
justify this hellish mistake.
Waiting day-to-day to hear some news,
To see if your body were strong enough and which outcome
it would choose.

That was shortly after the 2011 New Year,
I still remember *that* day crystal clear.

The best news I received was March/April time,
When your brother messaged me saying you'd woken up
and I knew you'd be fine.
I was so happy. I sent you well wishes in a photo of Billy
and me with a huge smile,
He replied, "She's doing well, but her recovery will be a long
while."

You were doing amazing I could not have been prouder of
your strength and courage to pull through,
You couldn't speak, you communicated with your eyes, he
added, "when you saw the photo you smiled too."
I cried tears of joy that day, and mentally sent you positive
vibes through,
There were so many things I wanted to tell you.

You kept fighting, and then disaster struck,
Your brain needed more time to heal, and multiple seizures
shook.
You were medically induced back into the coma and sent
peacefully to sleep,
It was three months of painful waiting, yet positivity we all
had to keep.

I strongly believed in you, that I would get my best friend
back in your own time,
When I received the news you had died, my world stopped
moving and I think everyone's heart broke, not just mine.
You tried, you fought, and I can say you did your best,
But I was grieving, I was angry, that someone had put you
to rest.

I felt robbed for you; I wouldn't accept it. I was in denial for
years,
I've lost count of how many times I've broken down into
tears.
The reassurance I received was that you were well looked
after and they tried everything and more,
That was enough passion for me to bottle in my own job as
a nurse as it had dwindled slightly before.

You never saw me qualify; you heard me moaning about my
training and how much I wanted to quit,
Waiting all those months, I'm not joking; my grades took a
hit.
Since I have qualified, I have released my passion and
emotion and shown it through the way I care,
As everyone deserves the best, just like you received all the
way over there.

I miss you, my friend, it's obvious, I wish you were here,
I'll spend today remembering you and maybe shed a happy
tear.
Do you remember Billy as a pup, and I showed you him on
webcam, you said, "Billy Paw?"
He curled up to sleep on my lap and boy did he snore.

That little pup is a big lad now Sofie two arms to hold,
But he has been my rock over the years, with a loving heart
of pure gold.
He sits and snuggles up to me when I speak of you,
His twitchy ears listen, and I know he misses you too.
He has caught so many tears over the years that I have
shed,
You should see the puzzled looks he gives me when they
drip on his head.

We both miss you, our dearest friend, every single day,
We are lucky to have had you in our lives. We treasure the
moments in our hearts where we know they will stay.
Not many people can say they literally have an Angel as
their best friend,
But now we bid you goodbye, sweet dreams, continue to
watch over us as we bring this poem to an end.

# Michael

Here's a little story about my best friend, Mike,
He lives in Aylesbury, where he loves to ride his bike.
A charming young man who's become a dear friend,
A new friendship that has grown, where my previous had
end.
We put rules in place right from the very start,
He knew I was gay and couldn't have my heart.
He knew if he tried anything, it would be a mistake,
As we value our friendship and wouldn't want it to break.

His first nickname was Cheeky Chappy,
As he always makes me laugh and feel happy.
He has plenty of qualities, I could tell you, but the list is
too long,
Looking for a flaw is even harder, as nothing he does is
wrong.
He's like a brother that I never had,
Who winds me up - Oh, so bad?
He may be almost six feet tall,
But his nickname for me is dwarf, as I am so small.

He is a great listener, caring and fun,
The only guy I've met where I don't want to run.
Nearly eight years of friendship that I do treasure,

Chatting to him is always a pleasure.

I can open up and tell him what is on my mind,

He will sit still and listen and a solution he will seek to find.

We have tackled through times both good and bad,

Even when we thought we had completely gone mad.

Hours we will spend chatting over the phone,

Having a best friend like Michael, I know I'm never alone.


All I want for him is to be happy, find a girl who makes him smile,

Anyone less than perfect, I'll make her run a mile.

It is a poem I cannot end, as it is a friendship forever growing,

But I cannot leave this without you knowing.


Thank you for everything you have done, the past, present and future too,

It is an absolute honour knowing my best friend, is you.

# Robyn

Thirteen years ago, I hopped on crutches into the common
room, where I screwed my knee,
Here at Wath Comprehensive I first met Robyn. What an
amazing friend she turned out to be.
Sat in our separate circles, her head in a book,
Occasionally to make conversation, up she'd look.

During A-levels, I had *gaydar*. She flashed up; I knew she
was gay,
I take the piss now. She found this out years in the future
one day.
Robyn's a bright lass, with one hell of a brain,
I knew she'd succeed in life and attend University when our
time came.

I used to think at sixth form she was incredibly quiet. I got
that wrong,
We instantly connected over our mutual love of *Friends* and
random outbursts of song.
We lost touch after college as we went in a different
direction,
You'd have guessed wrong if you'd have thought that would
have broken our connection.

She remembers seeing me in Meadowhall, Vue cinema,
In all honesty, this memory is foggy, and I cannot
remember.
We exchanged numbers once again, and we kept in touch,
Lots of phone calls and messages, catching up, as we had
missed so much.

It was during her time in Uni she told me she realised she
was gay,
I said I know; you should have seen her face; she didn't
have a clue what to say.
Erm...but...what? How?
*Gaydar* sweety, but I am glad you're up to speed now.

You could have told me Laura and saved me from months
of confusion,
Ok, you tell me how I'd have slipped that one into
conversation.
Oh yeah...Now I see,
Oh yeah...That was me.

Now, that was out. We both had a rough ride of
relationships that were quite bad,
We have both lost our heads and questioned are we mad?
We have both hit rock bottom and helped each other by,
Answering each other's questions when we get stuck on
why?

During these times, we were on call for each other, stay
awake chatting or texting,
Until our minds settled to a point where we would be
sleeping.
We always found our strength again after this session,
We got our fight back to teach life a lesson.
This is where we became *Musketeers* two for one,
We kept fighting our battles over the years until we have
won.


We did all sorts together, Cinema, Pubs, food, and a walk
around Rother Valley,
On this day, we took Billy and Jimmy.
They were only puppies and would not walk the whole way
round,
They just laid there panting, tired on the ground.
We each picked them up and carried them the rest of the
way,
It was an unsuccessful walk that day.


The day Kirsty met my two little boys,
They were excited and wagging and making such a noise.
She loved them both and said, so cute and great fun,
Good job, you hit it off as you got promoted to God-Mum.

Robyn, when we sat in Mum's garden eating an ice pop,
They wanted some real food, not from the pet shop.
I remember meeting Robyn's dog Stan for the first time, not
knowing he liked fur,
He swung off my gilet hood. She yelled, "STAN! That's not
how you're supposed to greet her."
What a lovely dog he was so charming but wappy,
I used to love seeing him; we were all smiles, laughing, and
happy.

I don't think we ever went to Pride just the two of us,
Before that, you introduced me to Kirsty, your missus.
Former Kirsty Wiles, now Mrs. Fisher,
Robyn's face is full of smiles, and you are perfect together.

We went to jewellery shops to buy Kirsty's engagement ring,
I laughed so hard, ripped you to pieces, you were so
nervous you were sweating.
We ended up in Las Iguanas mulling it over,
It was nice to see you in a state. I could see how much you
love her.

It's not the only time you have been in a fluster,
We went shopping for her birthday gift when you first got
together.
Trust me, Kirsty, this girl puts thought into every gift she
buys,

I've had the stress of it all, Love! Seen it with my eyes.
She knows I am joking as I love you really,
Just a picture that Kirsty never sees, but now she can clearly.

Your hen night, best night ever,
We drank and ate. Felt like I danced forever.
Next day you both felt it with a partial heavy head,
Up bright and early, Hayley and I, we went for breakfast instead.

Your wedding was a perfect day,
Robyn, I've never seen you in a dress. You both looked stunning, I must say.
I was happy for you both, holding back tears, so I didn't cry,
As stupid me forgot to pack tissues and my makeup to reapply.
It was your happiest day, but it was also for me,
As the two *Musketeers* finally became three.

I don't believe you know your importance. You're more than just friends for life,
You know your mission, VET the girl, one day I will be settled like the both of you, happy with my wife.

The three *Musketeers* we march on,
Ticking off crazy outings one by one.
Manchester Pride, oh my, can you remember?
We drank so much, midday the both of you finally surfaced
thanks to that hangover.
We had good food, drink, and cheesy pop music,
After that weekend, I think we all felt a bit sick.


When we went to Leeds daytime drinking playing Gay or
Not,
Kirsty thrashed us both the waitress in Las Iguanas. Now
she was hot.
We strolled to Revolucion de Cuba, and your look of
surprise,
You said music is good, live band where? I said, right in
front of your bloody eyes.
OOOOOH! Let's get to the bar,
A few cocktails later, a cheesy dance in Viaduct Show bar.
We got on the train, and Robyn and Kirsty ordered KFC,
I was absolutely knackered and tipsy. It was bedtime for
me.
That was one of the first outings the *Musketeers* had,
You see, folks, not all our trials have been bad.

When I bought my house, you both visited to see if I'd settled in,
I made you both nachos. You loved that greeting.
Later, it was a BBQ in the summer, and it was so hot,
We ate our body weight. There was plenty leftover; I begged please just take the lot.

Most recently though, you've been my rock as I've travelled through hell,
When I felt trapped and lost, it was the both of you that I'd tell.
You're helping me to bounce back from that heavy fall,
I want to say I love you both dearly, thank you, I salute you, "All for One, And One for All!"

# Something I Wrote for Your Funeral

A holiday in Spain was where we met,
I met Sofie, a girl I would never forget.
After a week, our time came to an end,
But I left Spain with a new best friend.

She helped me through, when Jonathan died,
She sat and listened, gave me a shoulder where I cried.
She was the type of girl who'd do anything for you,
Had a heart of gold, which was genuine and true.

She was a happy girl who always wore a smile,
Who would ride her bike mile upon mile?
Sofie was a friend I hold so dear,
I really wish she were still here.

She believed no matter how big a problem, there's always a
solution,
She went on to make me an elongated new year's
resolution.
"You are going to pass your driving test,
You're not just going to be a nurse; you're going to be the
best.
You like to do things that make your life worthwhile,
I bet you cannot ride your bike for 24 miles."

I laughed it off as she knows what I am like,
Off I went and jumped on my bike.
It was uphill, tough, and caused me so much pain,
In my mind, I saw you smiling and laughing again.

An angel in Heaven I believe you will be,
Who will continue to watch over me?
I still have the Angel stone you bought me in Spain,
When I hold it, all my memories come flooding back again.

You have left footprints in my heart,
Although we are miles apart.
I know we cannot speak every day,
The time we spent together, I wouldn't have had it any
other way.

Echte beste goede vriend,
You are an incredibly good friend, who I will love until the
end.
Every night I will look for the star that shines so bright,
I say goodbye, sweet dreams, and sleep tight.

# Two Months On

Two months today, you were laid to rest,
God took away someone who knew me the best.
Since then, I have tried to listen to our song,
Stay Another Day, but I end up turning it off because I
cannot stay strong.
6th of November, your birthday is coming up. I don't know
what I'll do,
We'd made plans to celebrate it, me you and your family
too.
As each day goes by, I miss you so much it hurts me inside,
To a point where I want to go and cry and hide.
Instead, I carry on with half a smile and walk tall,
Imagining that you never went away at all.
People tell me that time will heal,
Now, it isn't changing how I feel.
Even the good memories are causing me such pain,
One day I'll think of them, and I will smile again.

Sweet Dreams, my Angel

# Grief

Why is it that grief comes crashing back like a wave?
And reminds me of your life they could not save.
When days are good, I feel like I've moved on,
When they are bad, I realise you have gone.
I keep writing my poems to keep you alive,
Even then, they aren't that good because you never survive.
It's like I'm stuck in a nightmare, walking around,
All I can hear is your voice and laughter. It is your sound.
Some days I feel like you're right there beside me,
Then I question how can that be?
Some people say some tears never dry,
I think this is the case, so I might as well just cry.
There is no point holding back, as it is not going to end,
As this pain is torture, losing your best friend.
It seems I've lost motivation to do anything today,
All I want to do is curl into a ball and hideaway.
You used to pick me up when I felt like this,
That is why I cannot move forward as it is you that I miss.
The last words you said to me was, "I love you and thank
you for everything,"
You were dealing with your Grandma's death but still sent
my heart hammering.
We were as strong as an Ox, and we dealt with everything
together,

We could face any dilemma, no matter the weather.
There are times where I feel so alone and no one to turn to,
So, I deal with it myself as it used to be you.
One day these poems will be full of laughter and shared
memories we had,
We had some cracking ones, and none of them bad.
Right now, I'm still fighting to get a grip and my life back on
track,
All I want right now is my wish to come true, to have you
back.
Twenty is no age to go. I just hope you went with dignity
and peace,
Not in pain and unease.
I knew if I were by your side, I wouldn't have kept it strong,
I would have held your hand and stayed awake all night
long.
Although in a coma, I'd have spoken to you whilst you'd
sleep,
I wouldn't have been able to cover the tears throughout a
silent weep.
There's one thing I want to say, and it's for everything you
do,
I love and miss you more each day, but I'm saying a
massive thank you.
For everything you helped me with when you were here,
My New Year's resolutions you'd set me every single year.

Your continuous belief in me and that you said I'd do well,
You weren't wrong Sofie, because time really did tell.
I just wish you were here so you could see me now,
To show you that I did make it, but I have no idea how.
My Angel in the sky wearing the sun as her smile,
Thank you for the best five years; you made my life
worthwhile.

# Happy 21st Birthday

Today is your 21st Birthday, that we had planned to
celebrate,
But as we both know, God couldn't wait.
He's taken the girl who knew me the best,
And ensured she is peacefully sleeping and is at rest.
Today has been hard. I felt like my hearts tearing in two,
Partly because I remember the last conversation, I had with
you.
I know! I know! Nice things were said,
I should remember them and smile, but it hurts me
instead.
I hope you don't mind I cannot celebrate today,
As all I'm wishing for is that you could stay.
Gone too soon, we had distance before, but now feels far,
I'll be looking at the moon and wishing on that star.
Tonight, I'll light my candle and send you a prayer,
And I know that My Angel will be smiling up there.

# First Christmas

My only wish for Christmas is for you to be here with me,
Instead, you're the Angel sat on the top of our tree.
When I look outside my window, you're the star that shines
so bright,
The one I send my prayers too, every single night.
You really are a gift from Heaven, that returned but not by
choice,
I guess your family and my love couldn't drown out God's
beckoning voice.
Christmas is a time of laughter, family fun, and cheer,
Although you're not here to celebrate it, I won't shed a tear.
It's been a few months now since you went away,
Positive things have happened, and I felt you near me on
those days.
It gave me a sense of warmth, strength, and courage that
helps me to carry on,
But I think you should help your family now as this year
will be a tough one.
If I could give you one last gift, it would be a hug, and I'd
hold you for a while,
When we'd part, it would be with a great big smile.
On Christmas Day, I'll light a candle whilst thinking of your
name,
And hope to visualise you again, whilst staring at the flame.

I made you a promise that you'll have me as a friend for life
and look I'm still here,
Keep watching over me, guide me, and help me to celebrate
the New Year.

# Questions

Since your death, I went to the cinema to see a flick,
My oh my, what a tragedy they'd pick.
It was about a girl in a car crash, in a coma, who loses her memory,
I cried from beginning to end in absolute agony.
When I thought I'd moved on and dealt with things,
The utter shock and upset this film bring.
To be fair, *The Vow* was a good film, and I saw it through,
It brought back painful memories of the accident that caused the death of you.

I went through a mixture of emotions and questions that will never be answered,
After being in a coma, if I were stood in front of you, would you have remembered?
If I started to speak, would it have sparked a memory, good or bad?
Would you have remembered the dreams that you always had?
IF you had completely woken up, how would I feel and deal with seeing you that way?
You may not have known who I was; then we'd have nothing to say.
Almost a year has passed, and how do I feel?

Well, your death happened. I've accepted that it's real.
The Beyoncé song *Halo* was playing on the radio in Dad's
car the other day,
I listened to a different song on my iPod and looked the
other way.
Not because listening to it causes me any pain,
Just the words that are sung make me wish to see you
again.
To be honest, no matter how much time I'm given, I'll never
completely heal,
You were my best friend who knew my thoughts and how I
feel.
You're not just the past, the present, you're my future too,
You'll stay in my heart, be my Angel in Heaven, and keep
guiding me through.

# The Future Scares Me

When I think of the future, it's a very scary place,
When I look into the future, it is missing your face.
I miss talking to you, as you'd be the first person to tell,
From achieving something worthwhile, or when I felt
unwell.
You would say something silly, just to make me smile,
I'd turn to you with my problems, and you'd never run a
mile.

We promised an everlasting friendship, a promise I will
always keep,
Although you're not with me now, you're in an eternal
sleep.
Milestones and big days are the hardest, and still, there's
more to come,
My feelings overwhelm me, and all I want to do is run.

I do plan on getting married, yet it's a day I kind of dread,
It'll be a day of happiness and excitement with a hint of
sadness instead.
My best friend, my bridesmaid, won't be there instead,
she's miles away,
You could argue I've gotten off lightly with the speech you
could say.

I remember this conversation all those years ago,
You said, "When I make my speech the deepest shade of red, you will go."
It would be a dream having you there,
Yet deep down in my heart, you'd be smiling, crying happy tears somewhere.


I miss having you around, and it sometimes makes me sad,
I cherished the friendship that we had.
I tell people hold onto friendships and don't take them for granted,
Ours shouldn't have ended so soon. It's not what we both wanted.
I listen to music often and your song,
I think of the words, and I know I cannot go wrong.


You are in my thoughts every day,
My dearest friend who was taken away.

# The Association Stage

Why is it whatever I see, read, or hear reminds me of you?
Whether it's a film, book, line in a soap, I associate with
you,
Then I think of you for the rest of the day.

Example, a character got a diagnosis, knew he'd leave his
girlfriend,
They'd made plans for the future, and it was so sad,
But before the end,
Can you remember the conversations we had?

January 2011 New Year Day, we were talking,
Just general stuff, your Grandma, and my Billy,
Then it got to the future and what road we'd be taking,
You said as if you're still thinking, I know mine silly.

That friendship we would cherish day and night,
The one that made us invincible,
Where we'd be still talking when were old and grey,
Probably still listening to our favourite song, Girls Aloud's
Untouchable.

Even when you were going round town, you'd check in,
Even if it was an email or instant messaging,
Whenever I saw it pop up on screen, you'd know I was
smiling,
These are the things that I am missing.

Given the chance there are some things I'd love to tell you,
When you were sleeping, Billy climbed the stairs, for the
first time,
You did say it wouldn't be long, so true,
He sprints up, could choose any room, but guess which,
mine.

Not long after you died,
I went 'back home' to Spain,
In September, I finished my nurse training, and I qualified,
You supported me the whole way and wanted you to see it,
what a shame.

Billy has a little brother now called Jimmy,
He is so mischievous and cheeky but so entertaining,
He is our newest addition to our family,
His mannerisms are just like yours; it's like you're still here
and living.

I still take that stone you got me to work each day,
It did bring me luck in my interview,
It's a comfort thing, I know you're close by, and you'll stay,
So, I'll never lose my memories of you.

Losing one best friend is hard enough, but I have lost two,
In the space of less than two years,
But I managed to keep it together and pull through the
pain and tears.

Finally, when you were planning your 21st birthday,
When I said I might not be able to make it,
I was already planning to fly on over, so I'd be there on that
day,
I wanted to surprise you! As if I'd miss it!

Not a day goes by when I wish you were here,
Although things have changed and life goes on,
You're a special friend I hold so dear,
Do not worry; you're still my number one.

# 2015

I break my promises every year,
I keep promising that I won't shed a tear.
I break my traditions one by one,
Ever since the year, you were gone.

New Year used to be our favourite time of all,
Knowing we'd be planning it together was always a ball.
New Year's Eve, chatting about everything that's been and
gone,
New Year's Day, we'd make each other's resolution.

It seems naff writing about it now,
I know some people won't get it, yet it was special somehow.
2015 is nearly here...
I do wonder what challenges you'd have set me this year.
Would it be a challenge to make me smile?
I passed the bike ride, one 24 mile.
Would it be something to give me a fright?
Stay in a haunted house overnight.
I could never predict what you might say,
It was so random; I wouldn't have had it any other way.

Bet you thought the decisions I made were bad,
When you were watching, I bet I drove you mad.
The good things have flourished and are living on,
If I could see your smile, I bet it's the big one.

You left me to make my resolutions, so let's see,
What would be a good few for me?
I will reawaken your spirit and go to some clubs and dance,
Be grateful that you aren't making me listen to trance.
I will always stay positive every day,
And kick the negatives faraway.
I may make some commitments, some big and some small,
But I'll take it day by day. I've only got a year after all.

I am watching the fireworks light the sky, right near your
star,
Deep down, I know you aren't that far.
This year I'll make a wish especially for you,
2015 is here; Happy New Year, be My Angel, and keep
guiding me through.

# Happy 28th Birthday - My Angel

Happy 28th birthday to my dearest friend,
Every year hugs, kisses and well wishes I send.
I feel we were robbed as again you're not here to celebrate it,
You missed your 21st, crikey that would have been a smash hit.
Trance music, dance, singing, and drinking,
Surrounded by your friends and family would guarantee you smiling.

Losing my best friend in tragic circumstances was such a shock,
I never imagined how my world was going to rock.
Time has passed seven years; I believe it is now,
Wounds haven't healed, and I don't imagine they ever will somehow.

As I am getting older, I actually feel your absence more,
Some days I'm still devastated as it is still raw.
I could have the worst day ever, and my mood would be rotten,
One simple thing you'd say, belly laughing all would be forgotten.

Another example, your best friend should always be there
on your wedding day,
Whenever, if ever, that would be. I could really laugh at the
speech that you'd say.
It would be the most embarrassing thing I'd hear in my life,
No doubt, I'd be blushing in front of my wife.


Remembering all of the advice you gave me through Uni
when I wanted to quit,
The belief you powered me with as you knew I'd do it.
I was crushed you never saw me graduate,
You'd have been straight on over here to help us celebrate.


Your death changed me, not always for the better,
Grief, anger, the pain I felt was written in poems, and some
in a letter.
I can look around and observe other people's friendships,
and I can smile,
Or I can completely look away, withdraw, and run a bloody
mile.
I find myself envious and sometimes jealous,
How bad does that sound? I am being serious.
I wouldn't wish anyone to go through losing their best
friend,
It is torture and a deep pain that will never end.

Some days I really need you here, and you're not,
I can still wait for a funny text and pretend that you forgot.
Having you as my best friend, I was never down for long,
Within five minutes, I was back to being strong.

You had some brilliant goals for your life and future,
It kills me you never got to achieve them, and that I would lose ya.
People say to me, Sofie was that friend that everyone dreams of having,
A gift, a strong friendship, "Untouchable" is what we'd be singing.

I will never forget the night before,
You came to me in a dream, and it doesn't hurt me anymore.
I was walking down a street; you were smiling through a window waving me in,
I crossed the road and into that building I went running.
Hands on my knees, I was panting,
I looked around; you were nowhere to be seen, I couldn't work out why,
Little did I realise then you were peacefully smiling and waving me goodbye.

I woke up to a message from your brother saying you'd
gone,
My blood froze inside my veins; I was still, you'd have
thought I was made of stone.
I lived at home, I was distant and hardly spoke for a good
year,
Tortured by emotions, loneliness, loss, and a great big stab
of fear.

I attended my placement pretty much like a zombie,
My mentor at the time was excellent; she was guiding me.
I wanted to quit, stop, fail, throw it all away,
You'd have haunted me and given me a lecture, so I decided
to stay.
I couldn't see a way forward; I was consumed by complete
darkness,
I was a right mess.

I felt better when I'd written a poem for your funeral, and
they loved it,
I couldn't attend, but I felt it did you justice.
I never got chance to thank your family for keeping me up
to date,
After your funeral, we'd cut contact; it was too late.
Every day I miss you, I want my friend back, I want you to
know,

Our friendship was strong, solid, pure gold; I promise to
never let it go.
Keep silently walking beside me, keeping me strong,
Knowing that is happening, I cannot go wrong.
One day you'll see my bubbly personality snap back,
With your guidance, once again, you'll get me back on
track.
Thank you for the fun times, advice along the way,
My dearest best friend Sofie, forever in my heart, you are
going to stay.

## Letters

Dear Sofie,

Merry Christmas and a Happy New Year,

Still finding it strange that you aren't here.

Every year those new year's resolutions we'd set each other,

Don't worry girly; I've set them myself now, you needn't bother.

They aren't as challenging as the ones you'd set me,

Sometimes I need it easy as you knew how hard they'd be.

My first one is to get back on my bike,

Repeat the one you set me before you died, what a bloody hike.

Decided to do it as a personal challenge in honour of your memory,

But hopefully, the pain will be much less than before as it was agony.

Number two is to keep smiling and have fun,

As you're not suffering now, and at peace, so that battle we won.

Number three, to keep doing what you believed I did best,

My nursing, so I'll work hard and continue to help the rest.

I can't think of a fourth, but you'd have picked something outrageous,

That put the shock expression on my face, then laugh as it was contagious.

New Year, my Achilles heel, as we'd planned to celebrate it together,

I'm at work; then, with my family, hopefully, I'll feel better.

I'll not be alone in my room, thinking of you,

I'll be partying all night, just like you used to.

I want to say there'll be no more tears, but this I cannot promise it,

As one minute, I am fine, and the next they'll hit.

You know you were my best friend who went away,

But you know your special place where you'll always stay.

With me forever by my side,

You know I won't run or try to hide.

I hope your family and friends will be okay this year,

Or if they secretly like me wish you were here.

Billy loves you and would give you his paw,

You'd be impressed as he'd give you much more.

He has stuck by me at all times since you left,

Sat on my knee whilst I wept.

Don't worry about us though, we're doing fine,

It's an honour to have you both best friends to call mine.

So kickstart next year lil lady, and let's do it in style,

If you're lucky, I'll write you in a little while.

Goodnight God bless my Angel, we will look for your star,

Seeing it again, I know you're not that far.


All our Love

Laura and Billy

# My Guardian Angel Replied

*Dear Laura and Billy,*

*Do you need me tonight, right now?*
*I've laid a straightforward path for you to follow.*
*You're having a hard time, that's damn right,*
*Your mind is overworking, and you're awake all night.*
*You're lost big time, with no sense of direction,*
*When I left you alone, this was not my intention.*
*You're my best friend, Laura, forever in my heart,*
*But watching you struggle is tearing me apart.*
*I need to be there on earth offering you my protection,*
*Not through a dream or writing you a poem like the rest of*
*your collection.*
*We were the strongest team, and we would beat it all,*
*We'd brush ourselves off whenever we'd fall.*
*We stood up tall, proud, so bold, and so bright,*
*Prepared for whatever was thrown at us, we were ready to*
*fight.*
*We celebrated our victories with laughter and fun,*
*Reminiscing our memories, listing everyone.*
*You're listening to my playlist; this is great to see,*
*It is endearing to know that you're missing me.*
*But come on! Shake a leg, or I'll come and haunt you too,*
*I'll try and help you right now, but I can't physically be with*
*you.*

*Stay focused and positive and live the life that you dreamt,*
*As you know, in a flash, mine went.*
*I must laugh at you sometimes; you're still very funny,*
*Especially your blonde moments and the Guinea Pig Bunny.*
*You haven't changed, and no you're not broken,*
*I'm telling you now, your best friend has spoken.*
*You think I am not listening to your conversations with Billy,*
*I'm figuring some sound advice to give you, silly.*
*You fry my brain, and you're driving me mad,*
*Yes! Some of your past decisions have been bad!*
*I've been wanting to give you the heads up, so you'd know*
*you'll be fine,*
*I just want the best for you all of the time.*
*So, jump over the hurdles, tackle them one by one,*
*I am telling you now, girly, your confidence hasn't gone.*
*Yes! You are the shy girl I saw way back when we first met,*
*I am telling you now; you're not at your best yet.*
*You're ambitious, determined, and a huge achiever,*
*What did I tell you during University? I am a strong believer.*
*I just knew you'd do it; I am so proud,*
*I wish you could have seen me cheering you on. Man! I was*
*so loud.*
*My advice to you, Laura, my dear,*
*Is clear.*
*Walk tall, be strong, always smile and be bold,*
*Have no regrets about anything when you're old.*

*Ha-ha! When you're old, whereas I passed in my youth!*
*Sorry! Off on a tangent, how uncouth!*
*Where was I? Open your eyes and embrace every*
*opportunity,*
*Ensure you choose wisely the ones that'll make you happy.*
*I'll remain beside you, every single step of the way; I'll have*
*you know,*
*The day we meet again, I will say I told you so.*

*I Miss You Too*
*Lots of love from your best friend*
*Your Guardian Angel Sofie*

*P.S There is one little thing I also ask of you; it will be a*
*struggle, this I know,*
*Stop torturing yourself, and please let me go.*
*I will remain here guiding you your whole life and helping*
*you through,*
*And Billy, of course, my furry friend, I love you too.*

# Millennium Wheel – written aged 10

*Hi, I'm called the Millennium wheel,*
*I'm made of steel,*
*That's why I am called,*
*The millennium wheel.*

*I go round and round,*
*Never touch the filthy ground,*
*People smirking, men are working,*
*While I'm going round and round.*

*Parents are shouting, very loud.*
*Children on outings,*
*Going round and round.*
*People having picnics,*
*Eating chocolate biscuits,*
*While I'm going round and round.*

*Very bored am I,*
*Never tell a lie,*
*While butterflies fly,*
*Or else you will be,*
*In a big scrummy pie.*

*Are you listening?*
*I'm talking to you,*
*You better change that attitude,*
*Or else you will be in a very bad mood.*

*If you be good,*
*Your parents will think you are,*
*A flower bud,*
*Instead of honey,*
*You'll get pocket money,*
*If you are good.*

*This millennium let there be,*
*Some chocolate and sweets,*
*For you and me,*
*Of course, don't forget about,*
*Your family.*

*Now I must go,*
*But remember not to lie,*
*Or you will be in,*
*A big scrummy pie.*

*Goodbye.*

## Afterword

People ask me what my beliefs are. I always find this an interesting topic of conversation. I believe in the afterlife. I believe in Guardian Angels. The flashback to Southall, I should not be here now. I don't know how I survived that one if it wasn't for someone watching over me.

I remember driving with Dad on the way to work one day. We were visiting Gran on the ward. I openly said to him, before I became a nurse, death used to scare me so much, the thought of dying, the process, the aftermath. Since I have been a nurse, death no longer scares me. What I see is painful for the loved ones around, and for us too. I see someone at peace, and that brings me such great comfort.

People expect medical staff to be able to 'deal with death,' much better than a layperson. As you can see, this is not true, especially when it is one of your own, you love, and you're close. We feel it just the same.

The poem I wrote was written in my head at Grandad's bedside, and I wrote it in the car. The Christmas before his death, we spoke about death and dying. It was an open conversation. He wanted me to promise him that he would pass as peaceful as his wife did, Gran. I made him that promise.

The problem I have, though, is letting go. It does take a good while for me, and I do not know why I am scared to do so. Sofie's was the hardest. It was unexpected, tragic circumstances. I could not help but hurt as I saw she was robbed of her life. My poetry helped me so much, but as you can also see, my poems will come to me when I am awake or when I am sleeping.

As for my two Lhasa Apso doggies, well, to all you dog lovers out there, you cannot tell me you don't wonder what they'd say if they had a voice and could speak to you?

We all do.

I have touched on raw subjects as well as trying to be quirky. My poetry has raised awareness and offered comfort to many. I hope that it has helped you too.

I hope you're not dizzy after your ride on the Millennium Wheel.

Thank you, x.

*I would love for you to follow me ...*
Twitter @LauraFitton2
Instagram - @laurafitton